Dane Love is the author of numerous book … in particular. He was born in Cumnock but now lives in the countryside near Auch… e, who fought for Bonnie Prince Charlie at the battles of Prestonpans and Cul… gical and Natural History Society, he is also the Honorary Secretary of th… ation and a Fellow of the Society of Antiquaries of Scotland. He works as a P… . In his free time, he enjoys travelling around Scotland with his … children, visiting historic sites and doing research.

Rev Alexander Peden's grave before the erection of the 1891 monument.

Title Page and Back Cover: Ordnance Survey Six Inch Map of Cumnock of around 1855.
Following Page: A view of Townhead Street, looking west.

CONTINENTAL
UPHOLSTERER
LAG 290

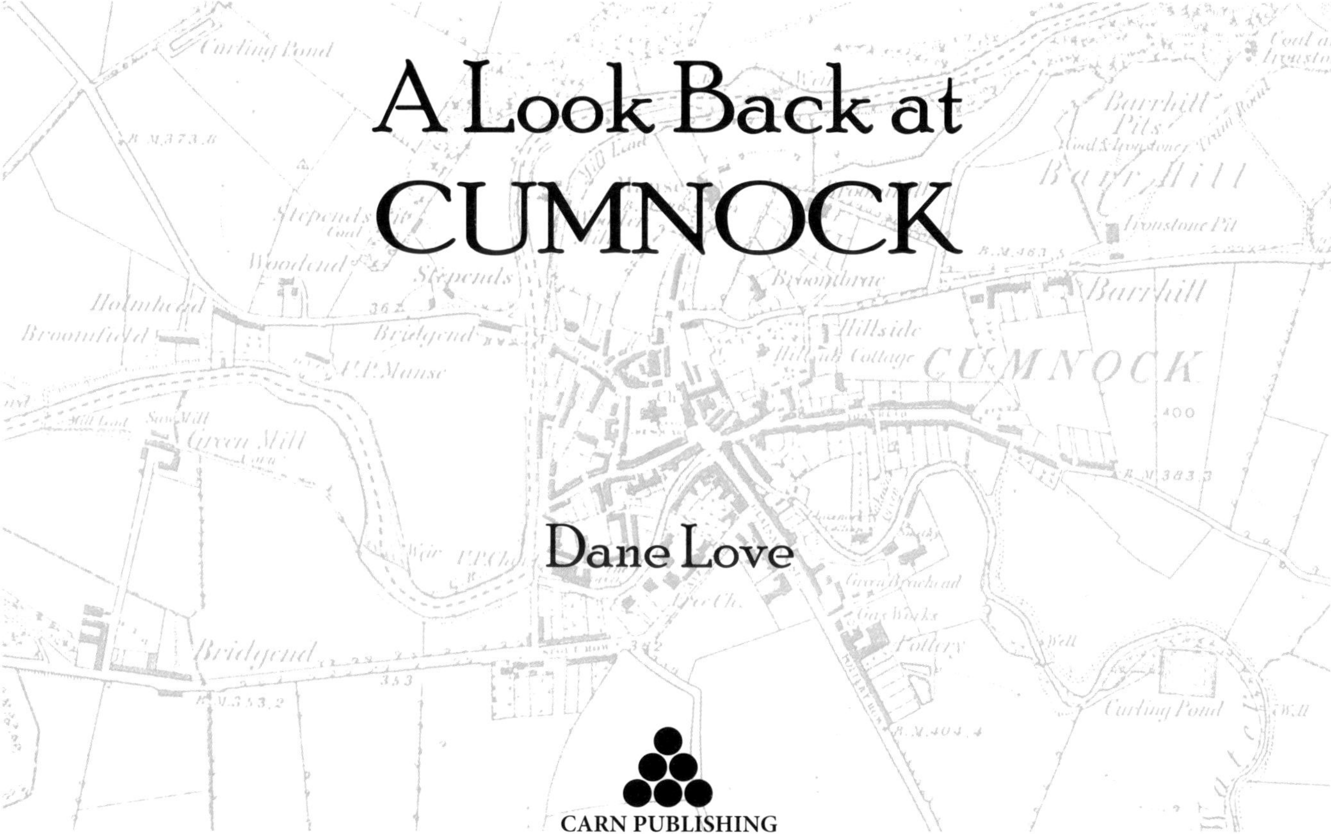

A Look Back at CUMNOCK

Dane Love

CARN PUBLISHING

First Published in Great Britain, 2010.

ISBN – 978 0 9567550 0 1

Published by Carn Publishing,
Lochnoran House,
Auchinleck,
Ayrshire, KA18 3JW.

www.carnpublishing.com

Printed by Bell & Bain Ltd.,
Glasgow, G46 7UQ.

Introduction

The small town of Cumnock lies in a hollow of the rolling Ayrshire countryside, where the Lugar and Glaisnock waters meet. An old town, there has been a village on this spot for centuries, enhanced in status in 1509 when the community was created a Burgh of Barony, allowing it to hold its own markets. From that time onward, Cumnock began to grow. There were five annual fair days – the most important being that held on the first Thursday after the 6 March, which was a notable feeing fair, the men of the parish hiring themselves out to the local farmers for the next year's labour. Originally, market day was every Thursday.

The name is difficult to explain, and has varied from 'the meeting of the waters', from the Celtic *cumar oich*, to the 'little shrine', from the Gaelic *cumanag*.

The parish of Cumnock, which was the same extent as the barony, was divided into Old and New Cumnock parishes in 1650, but this was annulled in 1667. In 1691 the parish was again split, and has remained so to this day. Old Cumnock parish extends to 14,209½ acres, but parts of the town in the Holmhead area are built within Auchinleck parish.

The oldest part of the town is centred on the Square, where the Old Parish Church stands. At one time this was surrounded by a graveyard, occupying what is now the public open area of the Square. At that time, the public roads took routes around the centre of town, along what are now back lanes, such as Bank Lane and Tower Street (at one time known as Back Street). The Square only became the public market place around 1768, when the graveyard was closed, a new cemetery having been opened on Barrhill Road around 1756, and the centre of town opened to public transport.

The local lairds were for many years the Dunbar family, who held the Barony of Cumnock, but in the late sixteenth century the Dunbars sold up and much of the parish eventually became the property of the Earl of Dumfries. At one time there were three castles in the parish – Terringzean, Leifnoreis and Borland, of which only Terringzean survives in ruins, within the policies of Dumfries House. It was anciently a seat of the Craufurd family. Dumfries House itself replaced the old castle of Leifnoreis, also a seat of the Craufurds.

Borland Castle was located near to Borland farm, on the road to New Cumnock. Of it, which was owned by the Hamiltons then Montgomeries, nothing remains on site.

Over the centuries, the parish of Old Cumnock has been divided into smaller landholdings, other estates being located at Garrallan, Glaisnock, Borland, Skerrington and Logan. Today, there are no landed proprietors left in the parish, Dumfries House and its surroundings being sold in 2007 by the Marquis of Bute to the Great Steward of Scotland's Dumfries House Trust, which operates it as a visitor attraction and agricultural estate.

Mining has played a major part in the history of Cumnock, though the deep mines have long-since closed. Most of the mines were for coal, although ironstone was also wrought on a smaller scale, some of the old mines such as Townhead, Shankston, Barrhill and Stepends, being located within the present extent of the town. The last major mine in the parish was at Whitehill, near Skares, which closed in 1965, although opencast surface mines have excavated coal across much of the parish since that time. Today, the connection with mining is dying and, apart from a few coal bings, there is little to hint at the parish's mining history. A memorial to the miners who lost their lives deep underground is located in the shopping centre.

Other industries have come and gone over the centuries in the town, and no doubt will continue to do so. At one time the manufacture of snuff boxes was a popular trade, Cumnock being noted as the place where the 'secret hinge' was first made. However, the trade gradually moved to Mauchline. The Cumnock Pottery manufactured basic earthenware goods for many years, latterly being noted for its 'Auld Scotch motto ware', on which local couthy sayings were written, such as 'It's nae loss what a frien' gets.' The pottery closed in 1907, but the earthenware is still collectable.

The manufacture of agricultural machinery was carried on in a smallish scale, and weaving and woollen manufactories existed. In more recent years, clothing, from denim to knitwear was made, and the manufacture of shoes and boots employed a number of people. Carpet manufacture took place in the post war years, and some transport manufacture has occurred, from the short-lived Stonefield cross-country vehicles to the current manufacture of fire engines.

Other major events in the history of the parish include the Covenanters, the seventeenth century Presbyterians who took a stance against the imposition of Episcopacy on them. In the parish four Covenanting martyrs were interred, some executed in the Square. Buried in the Barrhill, at the site of the gallows, were David Dun, Simon Paterson and Thomas Richard. Also buried in the Barrhill cemetery was Rev Alexander Peden, one of the most significant Covenanting ministers. John MacGeachan, another martyr, lies buried in a field outside Logan.

In 1866 Cumnock became a police burgh, which allowed the formation of the burgh council. This operated the local domestic services until the burgh councils were abolished at regionalisation in 1975. The council was progressive in developing the town, and numerous council houses were erected around the historic core. Many of these were built to re-house miners from the old rows at Garrallan and Skares. Similarly, the communities of Logan, Craigens and Netherthird were erected in the post-war years to take a growing population.

The town has continued to grow, but at a steadier pace, and most recent building work has been private housing developments. The largest is Holmhead, most of which is located within the parish of Auchinleck, but which is attached to the town. Other private houses have been erected at various locations around the town.

The by-pass road to the west of the town was opened in 1992, virtually locking the town between it and the railway line. A considerable segment of the town centre, between Townhead and Glaisnock streets, was redeveloped in the 1970s, with little success and the loss of many attractive old buildings. Future proposals to redevelop the town centre hope to amend what ripped the heart out of the old town. Linked with the developments proposed for Knockroon, on Auchinleck Road, there is a growing awareness of the town's heritage, both built and social, and tourism is being encouraged.

Woodroad Park

The Woodroad Park is located in the glen created by the Lugar Water. To either side of the river the banks are wooded and these, together with a stretch of grassland that was formerly part of Templand Mains farm, was purchased in 1935 for £500 to create a park. In 1937 Lady Talbot de Malahide, owner of Auchinleck estate, gifted the former Stepends pit site and bing to add to the park. The view shown was taken in the late 1930s, the vantage point being the Strawberry Bing, so called because wild strawberries grew on the slopes. The bing was formed by the Templand Mine. In the lower part of the picture the fountain can be seen, with children playing in the water. This was later filled in and turned into a flower bed. Only the foreground is of the park, the open field in the background being the Glebe, the fields that formerly surrounded the Manse. Just left of the centre is the Manse building itself, an old house of around 1750, but which was extended in the nineteenth century. The manse was sold in the 1950s and the grounds were purchased by Cumnock Town Council. Sixty houses were built on the fields.

The Woodroad Park has been the centre of Cumnock's leisure activities since it was opened until the present. Here the famous Cumnock cyclists' rally was held from 1938 until the 1950s, the Queen visited in 1956, and the Carnival had its finale there, the carnival queen being crowned in the park. The open air swimming pool was built in 1936, and it served the town until 2003, when the new indoor pool was opened at Broomfield. The tennis courts were opened in 1936 by Mrs R. D. Hunter. For many years there was a caravan and camping site at the top of the park, Cumnock being a popular place for holidaymakers. In 2007 the Woodroad Regeneration Forum started work on restoring the park to its former glory. New play equipment was installed, and the carnival was revived in 2010.

Garrallan House

The house of Garrallan was the mansion on a small estate which at one time included farms such as Changue and Crofthead. A fairly traditional and plain building, it has been added to slowly over the years. On the walls are a number of old carved stones with coats of arms and dates, including 1660 and 1868.

Probably the earliest reference to Garrallan as a single estate was in 1562 when a charter to the lands was granted by Sir Matthew Campbell of Loudoun, father of Sir Hugh Campbell, 1st Lord Loudoun, to Hew Campbell of Bogcoroch, a fairly close relative. Hew Campbell was a scion of the Campbells of Shankston, also a Cumnock family. Hew Campbell died in 1602 and the estate was inherited by his son, also Hew Campbell, who died in 1648. The second Hew's grand-daughter, Margaret Campbell, inherited, and she was married to George Douglas of Waterside, taking the estate to that family.

On the deaths of Margaret and George Douglas, Garrallan passed to their son, Hugh Douglas, his son, also Hugh, and then *his* son, Patrick Douglas (d. 1819). It was he who was making arrangements for Robert Burns to emigrate to Jamaica, where he was going to work as a book-keeper on his plantations, managed by a younger brother, Charles Douglas. Burns, of course, did not emigrate and remained in Scotland. On the death of Patrick the estate passed through the female line once more, to his daughter, Jane, who was married to Hamilton Boswell, a member of a branch of the Auchinleck family. Hamilton Boswell's father was John Boswell of Knockroon, the last Boswell thereof. Hamilton Boswell assumed the additional surname Douglas on marrying Jane.

John Douglas Boswell succeeded on the death of his mother in 1862. However, he died the following year and he had no issue. The estate then passed to his brother, Patrick Charles Douglas Boswell (1815-92), who is commemorated by a stained glass window in the Old Parish Church.

Garrallan estate was acquired by the Stevenson family, who had been tenants on Changue farm since 1870. The house was sold by the Stevenson family in 2003. Garrallan was restored in 2005 by Brian Allan Whyte, funeral director, but it has since been sold.

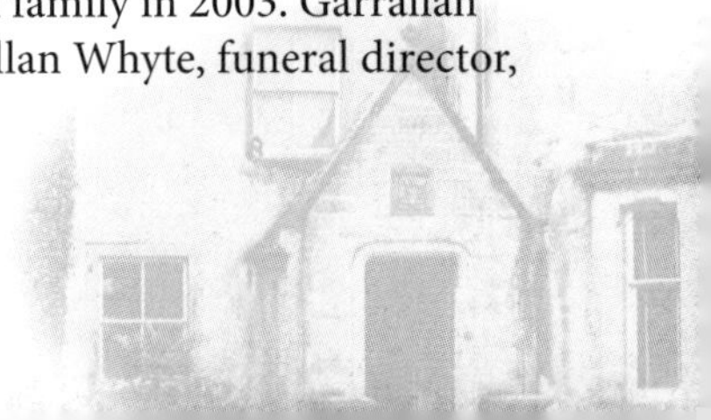

The Holm

This postcard view of the Holm across the Lugar Water was taken early in the twentieth century from a viewpoint just off Ayr Road. The three main buildings on the left are actually in what is known as Holmside, the buildings on the extreme right being in the Holm itself. Between the two roads is an open field, about five acres in extent, partially occupied by 1960s private houses. Twelve council houses were erected at the bottom of the Holm in 1956, just off the picture to the right.

The Holm Field was sometimes used for public events, amongst these being the impressive Drumhead Service, held on 18 February 1943 under the chairmanship of Rev Dr Selby Wright – 'The Radio Padre' – from Edinburgh. On that occasion King George VI and Major General W. R. Clutterbuck attended, witnessing the army carry out river-crossing exercises across the Lugar Water.

Behind the house on the left of the picture is Stepends Bing, here seen with a lack of foliage, for at the time the bing was still fairly fresh, the pit having closed in 1892 after having operated for 32 years. Holmside House (centre) was occupied by the local councillor and J.P., Samuel Galbraith (d. 1920). He was the owner of S. & A. Galbraith's grocery shop and wholesaler, a business founded in 1849. To the left of Holmside House are two large semi-villas. Linwood was at one time occupied by John Dick, schoolmaster. Another house was occupied by Dr James MacQueen, after whom MacQueen Avenue was named. Coilantogle was occupied by William Osborne Kay, who ran a chemist's shop in the Square in the early twentieth century, known as the Apothecaries' Hall. The manager of this shop later set up his own chemists in the Square as J. L. Galloway.

The gable and belfry of the Congregational Church building is seen to the right, erected in 1883. In front of it is a low building that formerly sat across Auchinleck Road from the church. This was formerly a row of five or six cottages named Bridgend. The building has been demolished and a modern bungalow occupies the site.

Swimming Pool

One of Cumnock's beloved resources, the swimming pool was officially opened in June 1936 by the Provost of the Burgh of Cumnock and Holmhead, Mrs Nan Hardie Hughes, who had made the original suggestion to build it. A total of 2,500 spectators gathered to witness the event. It was soon to be recognised as 'one of the finest inland open air swimming pools in Great Britain.'

Proposals for a pool had been made soon after the Woodroad Park was opened in 1935, though initially many of the residents opposed it. At length it was put to a vote and those who wanted a swimming pool won by 404 votes to 332. The hole in the ground for the pool was dug by hand, and horses and carts were used to carry away the earth and stones. The pool measured 100 feet by 45 feet, the depth varying from three feet six inches to ten feet deep. In total, the pool was filled with 200,000 gallons of water which was filtered and sterilised. Diving boards existed at the deep end. Although the pool was open-air, it was heated and it had the additional facilities of 'dressing cubicles, sprays' and a cafe. Visible in the centre of the photograph was a fountain, but this was to be shut off and removed at a later date.

The pool was a popular resort for locals and visitors to the town, early pictures of the interior showing a packed pool and viewing area. There was a tradition of the first person to be in the water when the pool opened for the summer season being gifted with a free season ticket for the remainder of the year, resulting in keen competition between young children. Many galas were held in the pool, and Cumnock Amateur Swimming Club was formed following a public meeting in the Town Hall on 17 March 1936. Cumnock Dolphin Amateur Swimming Club was founded in 1963. Latterly the pool suffered from the escape of water and spiralling costs meant that it became uneconomic to run. It was closed in 2003, before the new Visions swimming bath was opened at Broomfield on 9 October 2004.

Glaisnock House

The earliest reference we have to the old house of Glaisnock dates from 1586 when William Campbell of Glaisnock's daughter was married. A later member of the family was John Campbell of Glaisnock, who was fined £480 Scots in 1662 for supporting the Covenant. The estate remained the property of the Campbells for many years thereafter, until around 1730 when it was acquired by the Dicks followed by the Stevensons. The estate passed to the Allason family in 1797, a branch of the Allasons of Logan. Alexander Allason died in 1833 and was succeeded by his brother, James Allason.

Part of the present house was built around 1840 using what was described as 'a beautiful white freestone, from a quarry on the banks of the Lugar.' In 1855 the house was extended, the estate having passed to Captain Robert Campbell of Auchmannoch (in Sorn parish). The large additions are the part on the right of the picture, Campbell's arms being inserted over the doorway. In the early part of the twentieth century the house was let to various tenants, including the managing director of the John Brown shipyard in Clydebank followed by the owner of Workman, Clark & Co., shipbuilders in Glasgow.

Glaisnock House was acquired by Ayr County Council in 1949 and opened as a residential school on 15 September 1952, the first headmaster being John F. Gilmour. He was followed by Major John Weir DSO MA. The school was used as a rural school, teaching sons of farmers and others. The roll in 1952 was 89, of which 26 were boarders. In 1965 the roll was 135 pupils. In 1968 the school was upgraded to a four-year school. The school was closed in June 1973. The house was then converted into a residential outdoor centre, closing in 1996. Children from all over the former Strathclyde region came to Glaisnock for outdoor pursuits. From 2004 to 2007 the house was run as a centre for the arts, but the Glaisnock Trust, which operated it in association with Kilmarnock College, fell into financial difficulties, and the building was closed again, awaiting a new use.

Glaisnock Street Villas

This old postcard view of the top end of Glaisnock Street dates from before 1910. A series of large villas had been erected along the east side of Glaisnock Street from the old Pottery south towards the New Station. Among these houses are Viewfield, which dates from 1874, and Muirfield, designed by John Baird, founder of the institute that bears his name. John Baird, though a draper to trade, was also something of a keen architect and engineer, and some of his drawings survive.

Another house, known as Breezyhill, was erected by Adam Brown Todd (1822-1915), a local writer who wrote various books about the Covenanters *(Homes, Haunts and Battlefields of the Covenanters* and *Covenanting Pilgrimages and Studies)*, as well as numerous poems. A popular figure in the town, he was also editor of the *Cumnock Express* for a time. It was he who was responsible for instigating the erection of the memorial on the Barrhill to Rev Alexander Peden, the famous Covenanting minister, and the erection of a plaque at Lugar to William Murdoch. Todd was also a keen Burnsian, and presided at numerous local Burns' suppers. He often squabbled with James Keir Hardie in local politics. His grave can be found in the new cemetery.

In the centre of the picture can be seen a milestone, which indicates that Ayr is sixteen miles further on, and that Dumfries is 43 miles in the opposite direction. To the left, behind the railings and trees, is the Roman Catholic church of St John, which was erected in 1882 to plans by the London architect, William Burges. Most of the old railings and pillars that lined the street have now gone, residents of the houses having taken them away in many cases to allow access to park their cars, though many were initially removed as part of the war effort. The widening of the road on the left, in front of the photographer, is the entrance to Cairn and Car roads, the cameraman probably standing on the wall adjacent to the former station cottages, which were located in the gusset of the road, now the site of George MacTurk Court.

Glaisnock Viaduct & the Curling Pond

Cumnock is well known for its two viaducts, the larger crossing the Lugar Water, and this one, the Glaisnock Viaduct, crossing the Glaisnock Water. The viaduct was erected in 1872 by the Glasgow and South Western Railway Company as part of the line linking Ayr with Edinburgh. At the same time Cumnock New Station was opened, located at the top of Glaisnock Street, the site now occupied by George MacTurk Court. The viaduct is around 550 feet in length, and strides across the glen with thirteen arches, the tallest of which is 75 feet above the level of the water. Teams of Irish navvies erected the masonry, using timber scaffolding to support it.

The viaduct is properly known as the Glaisnock Viaduct, but in some old accounts it is named the Deil Stane Viaduct. This name comes about due to the fact that a large boulder in the glen below had a local tradition of being associated with the devil. Children used to claim that if you ran round the stone three times in an anti-clockwise direction, the devil would appear!

The railway line was closed in 1951, and after this the old line became a popular path. With the erection of the Barshare housing scheme from 1962 onwards, the path became even more popular, and is still used as a link between the two parts of the town.

In the foreground, just above where the Glaisnock Water flows past, can be seen the old Curling Pond. This measured around 260 feet by 150 feet, almost one acre of surface water, and was at one time a popular resort for the sport of curling in the cold winters. The pond was filled from the Glaisnock, and at the western end of it was a sluice which allowed the water to be released into the stream. Cumnock Curling Club was founded in the nineteenth century.

There were a number of other curling ponds in the parish, including one at the foot of what is now Holmhead Road, another at Woodhead, on Dumfries House estate, and smaller ones elsewhere.

DYERS

Looking West along Ayr Road

Ayr Road as a street dates from the late eighteenth century; previously the route from Cumnock to Ayr went from the centre of town at the Square down the Townfoot (now Tower Street) and across Dubb Ford to join the present Ayr Road. In 1780 a new road was made from Cumnock south towards New Cumnock (known as Glaisnock Street), and about the same time the new road from Glaisnock Street west to the Dubb Ford area was created. This view was taken from the upper floor of what was the Co-operative society building, in Glaisnock Street. The building on the right, with the window on the curved wall, was at one time occupied by a milliner, successively Miss Paterson, Mrs W. O. Kay and then the Misses Smith and MacCubbin. Mario Luni and his son Ernesto took over, converting the building into a restaurant and café, known as the Welcome Cafe. The building dated from 1873. It was demolished in the 1970s and the site remains undeveloped.

Prior to the 1873 building, this corner site was occupied by a toll house, a fee having to be paid to travel along Ayr Road. The toll cottage was a single storey building, the gate blocking Ayr Road unless the toll had been paid. The toll here was replaced by others at Bankend and one near to the Town Hall, tolls in general being abolished in 1878.

The building next door, outside of which is the horse and cart, was at one time the post office, prior to it removing to Lugar Street in 1911. With the arrival of the telephone to Cumnock in 1902, the exchange was built behind it. The post office was later occupied by A. F. Borland's ironmongery, latterly owned by Robert Leitch. For a number of years it has been an Indian restaurant.

On the south side of the street a series of large villas were erected on top of the banking, which was landscaped into gardens. The houses date from between 1857, when there were no houses here, to around 1900. Many of these houses still survive, important examples of Victorian architecture.

Dumfries House

The architectural gem of the Cumnock area and, indeed, one of the finest country houses of Scotland, is Dumfries House, which lies just to the west of the town in the middle of an extensive estate. The mansion was designed by the famous Scots architects, John and Robert Adam, one of their first major pieces. The house was built for William Crichton, the 5th Earl of Dumfries from 1754-59, one of whose lesser titles was Lord Crichton of Cumnock. It replaced the older Leifnoreis or Lochnorris Castle, of which nothing survives, not even a sketch. Lord Dumfries had originally wanted William Adam, the brothers' father, to design the house, but he died in 1748. Lord Hopetoun informed Dumfries that the Adams were up to the job, so he commissioned them on 24 April 1754. The estimate for building the house was £7,979 11s 2d, and the final bill for the completed house was just over this by a few pennies.

The house is shown from the south in this early twentieth century postcard. It had recently been extended, with additional blocks added behind both wings to plans by J. Weir Schultz, adding a ballroom and chapel. The main block of the house has its entrance at first floor level, reached by the fine flight of stairs. On the pediment are the arms of Lord Dumfries. The rest of the building is fairly plain, a magnificent example of Adam's Georgian work.

In 1814 the 7th Earl of Dumfries inherited the title and estates of the Marquis of Bute, and it became a secondary house on his extensive estates. For much of its life it was hardly occupied, leaving it as an untouched example of eighteenth century architecture. Leaving things alone even extended to the contents, which still has most of the original pieces of furniture specified by Adam for each room.

In 2007 the house was placed on the market by the 7th Marquis of Bute, and it was acquired before the contents were broken up and dispersed in a last minute deal by Prince Charles. Now owned by the Great Steward of Scotland's Dumfries House Trust, the house and grounds are open to the public.

Ayr Road & Crichton Memorial Church

This view of Ayr Road was taken looking north east along the street. On the immediate left is the magnificent Trinity Church building, one of the town's best examples of architecture. The church was the gift of Miss Crichton in memory of her father, Hew Crichton, and brother, Sheriff James Crichton. The first proposals for a new Free Church were made by the Crichtons in 1895. An Edinburgh architect, Duncan Menzies, was commissioned to draw up the plans for the church, and it appears to have been one of very few that he designed. Built of red sandstone, the church was erected between 1896 and 1899. The cost of the building was not revealed, but estimates at the time put it at around £10-12,000. Internally the church is embellished with fine stained glass, installed in 1906. Externally the building is distinguished by its 140 feet tall spire, one of the principal landmarks in the town. Rev John Warrick (1855-1931) was the first minister in the new church – he wrote the *History of Old Cumnock*, published in 1899. In 1949 the church was renamed the Crichton West Church, on the union with the old West Church in the Tanyard, and from 2006 has been known as Trinity Church.

To the right of the church building is a single-storey block which originally had three shop premises within it (38-42 Ayr Road). This block was erected at the same time as the church, and most likely was the work of the same architect. Originally the parish council had its chambers in the centre unit, the other two occupied by Gilmour's bakery and a solicitor's office. In 1963 the building was converted into one office, used for many years by Stevenson's Dairy Farms, but since 2008 has been occupied by Rosebud's craft and coffee shop.

The double-storey building behind the sandstone premises was in the nineteenth century Miss Ramage's School for Girls, but this closed in 1872. It was then converted into tea merchants before being converted into two shops, the frontage being extended to the street at that time. The basement of the old house was then converted into a pawnbrokers, Mr Kernahan moving there from the original premises at the Pawn Steps at the Square.

The Glebe & Barr Hill

From the top of Stepends Bing one could originally look over the younger trees at the town from various angles. This view, taken around 1900, is looking almost due east, the Bank Viaduct being an instantly recognisable object at the back left of the image. In front of it the small roadway led through the open fields to Templand Mains farm, which lies just behind the viaduct.

In the centre foreground is the old Sandbed Mill, which had certainly been in existence from at least the seventeenth century, and no doubt for centuries before. Up to 1692 the miller was Alexander Duncan, after which it was taken on by George MacGawn, followed by his son, John MacGawn. A weir across the Lugar Water directed water along the mill lade to the mill, rejoining the river just short of the Lugar Bridge. This weir was rebuilt in the 1700s, but it affected the flow of the Lugar which began to wash away part of the land on the north side, which was owned by James Boswell of Auchinleck, resulting in some animosity. In the nineteenth century the mill was extended, doubling its size, and it was converted into a woollen mill, but this was closed by 1908. The mill was latterly occupied by Ayrshire Bakeries, and then the burgh cleansing department's depot, but it was demolished and the site is now occupied by Warrick Court sheltered housing.

Above the mill in the picture is the old manse building, which still survives in Robertson Avenue. The oldest surviving portion may date from the mid eighteenth century, the larger block an addition of the nineteenth century. When it was closed as a manse it was converted into two houses. To the right of the manse can be seen Millbank House, built around 1860 and owned by the Livingstone family, grocers. In 1931 it was taken over by Cumnock District Council as their office. Above the manse the large house visible is Broomhill House, owned in the late seventeenth century by Lady Logan, but rebuilt and occupied by the MacKerrows and Bairds.

The Town Hall & Picture House

On the left of the picture is Cumnock Town Hall, erected in 1883 of red sandstone to plans drawn up by Robert Ingram. Proposals for a hall had been made a few years previously, and Lord Bute offered the council three possible sites – the Jail Field (which was located behind the old police station in Townhead Street), the site of White's old barn in Ayr Road, or the site that was selected – Glaisnock Street. Lord Bute gifted the ground and contributed £500 towards the fund. The cost of the building was expected to be £2,000. Three architects were invited to compete in a competition, the winner to receive the task of designing the new hall and to be paid 3½% of cost of construction. The hall was opened to the public in January 1885. The hall was still in debt ten years later, when a 'Grand Bazaar' was held with the intention of completing the fundraising to cover the cost, which was successful.

When it opened, the town hall became the hub of parish life, for here the council met in its chambers, dances and flower shows were held in the large hall, meetings and demonstrations in the Lesser Hall. During the wars it was often used for emergency accommodation and for billeting soldiers. When local schools required extra classrooms, the hall was often used.

Behind the large tree is the old Picture House, which was erected in 1913. In 1930 the 'talkies' arrived at the picture house for the first time, attracting greater audiences. The picture house closed in the early 1970s and was converted to a bingo hall. This too, was closed in 2007 and the building was demolished in 2010, despite it being one of the last Art Deco picture houses surviving in Scotland.

To the right of the Picture House is the façade of the Dumfries Arms Hotel, with the three dormer windows, one of the oldest buildings surviving in the town, originally founded on 25 March 1717 as the New Inn. It became the Dumfries Arms in 1840. Sir Walter Scott and Robert Burns were visitors at the inn.

Lady Bute's Hospital

The Bute Hospital was erected on the Barr Hill in a plot of almost two and a half acres, now occupied by Murray Court. The hospital was the gift of Gwendolyn, the Dowager Marchioness of Bute, to the town, and it was erected in 1882-3, opening in January 1883. The architect responsible was Allan Stevenson. Initially the hospital had ten beds and three cots for infants. It was extended in 1902, the work also by Stevenson.

The hospital was operated by the Sisters of the Sacred Hearts of Jesus and Mary and was fully equipped to deal with surgical cases. The beds were always filled, and though operated by the sisters, it was noted that the hospital was non-sectarian, 'the ministers of the patients can visit them at all times.' Visiting times for friends were limited to Thursdays and Sundays from two till four in the afternoon.

For the first 37 years or so, the cost of operating the hospital was met by the Bute family, but on 30 May 1920 they indicated that they would no longer be able to pay this. Local fundraising committees were then set up to cover the cost of maintaining the hospital's much-needed services, and funds were also received from local miners, who paid a regular sum from their pay, trade unions and other groups. A new committee of management was established on 4 November 1921, one of the longest-serving members being W. D. Wardrop of Rigg, chairman.

The Bute Hospital was operated on cottage-hospital lines, and its services were often required to treat injuries. Many miners who suffered by falls of stone underground were transported to the hospital for treatment and care.

With the arrival of the National Health Service and Hospitals Board in 1948, the hospital was closed in 1950 and health services were transferred to Ballochmyle Hospital, near Mauchline. The former hospital was then converted into a convent. Known as the Sacred Heart Convent, the nuns remained until the 1970s. The building was demolished soon after, and Murray Court houses were erected in the grounds, the site of the hospital being approximately where the central grassed area now is.

View from Stepends Bing

One of the classic views of Cumnock, this photograph was taken from the top of Stepends Bing, which still rises above the houses of Auchinleck Road. Today, trees have covered much of the bing, preventing so clear a view over the town. This image was taken early in the twentieth century. Four churches are prominent in the view – The Congregational Church of 1883 in the bottom left, the Old parish church of 1866 almost directly above it, the Crichton Memorial Church of 1899 with the tall spire, and the United Free Church of 1831 on the far right (now The Box House, bar and café, but the oldest church building surviving in the town).

Between the U.F. Church and the Congregational Church one can see numerous buildings along Tanyard Lane, all of which have been demolished, leaving the more open area we know today, forming the car park and bus stance. At one time this was one of the busiest parts of the town, with commercial premises and manufactories located here. Indeed, two large chimneys can be made out, that to the right being Galbraith's jam and preserve factory. Other industrial premises in this part of the town included John Andrew's factory (making aerated waters). The chimney just to the left of the viaduct (and left of the Dumfries Arms Hotel) was connected with the gasworks.

The building in the foreground with the hipped roof is Stepends House, probably erected in the late nineteenth century, after Stepends pit had closed in 1892. It was at one time the home of Robert L. Baird and then John Kerr, surgeon. In recent years it became the property of the Lewis then Andrew families.

The Holm is mostly undeveloped at this time, only four houses appearing in the picture. Beyond them, the rest of the holm was just that – a flat field by the side of the river.

At the end of the Holm can be seen the single storey Bridgend cottages, built alongside Auchinleck Road. A bungalow now occupies the site.

Shankston Cottage

This is a rare view of one of the old cottages that used to exist in the countryside around Cumnock. At one time there were a number of single buildings dotted around the town, most of which have been demolished when new building work has taken place. Shankston Cottage was located to the south west of the town, its site now occupied by the houses at the north-west end of Glenramskill Avenue. The cottage was a typical vernacular building of the early nineteenth century, at first glance reminiscent of Burns' Cottage in Alloway. The photograph was taken in 1948, which was shortly before the cottage was demolished. The two doors and chimneys indicate that there were in fact two dwellings here – in 1914 the houses were occupied by Robert Gilmour, a miner, and Hugh Barr, a ploughman.

Anciently Shankston was part of a small estate that was owned by the Campbells, the earliest reference to it being from 1488 when it was owned by John Campbell. These Campbells appear to have become involved in various local feuds. In 1512 Patrick Dunbar of Corsencon was murdered in Cumnock Kirk, for which Andrew Campbell was hanged. Others involved included Robert Campbell of 'Schankistoune' and his brothers, George and John, who were all put to the horn.

In 1601 George Campbell, son of the laird, was accused of being part of the feud between the Muirs of Auchindrane and the Kennedys of Cassillis. In 1612 when John Campbell succeeded to the estate he was ordered 'to big and repair ye mansioun place of Schankistoun, and eftir my deceis to duell yr. intill himself, leving all vrs. his roumes and duelling places, and to remane onlie in Schankistoun, becaus it is ye maist ancient duelling place.' Colonel John Campbell, son of James Campbell, 2nd Earl of Loudoun was the owner for a time. Col John Campbell was M.P. for Ayrshire from 1700-2. He died without issue.

The exact location of Shankston House is no longer identifiable on the ground, but it was in the vicinity of Shankston Wood.

A70
MUIRKIRK
A76
KILMARNOCK
A70
AYR
LIVE STOCK REMOVER
ARABIA
NIGHTS
OLD CUMNOCK

Cumnock Carnival 1950

This photograph shows a parade of floats passing up Glaisnock Street on Carnival day in 1950. Cumnock Carnival ran for many years before stopping in the 1970s due to a lack of organisers. It was revived in 2010 with considerable success, the last Carnival Queen, May Thompson (nee Richard), who was crowned in 1974, passing over the crown to the new queen, Rachel Milligan. In 1962 the queen was crowned by 'Miss World', Rosemarie Frankland.

A major part of the carnival was the parade of dressed lorries, which became significant examples of decoration. Various organisations and streets vied with each other to win the honour of being the best-dressed float, for many years Holland Crescent and Ayr Road being friendly rivals. The first float in the picture was that of the Old Cumnock Labour Party, complete with their banner depicting James Keir Hardie. The lorry used belonged to John Baird Transport, a long-established haulage contractor in the town, for many years based at a depot on the Barrhill Road.

The photograph, which was taken from the first floor of the Dumfries Arms Hotel, shows an impressive array of shops and commercial premises on Glaisnock Street. The ruin on the right was originally some cottages, adjoining Dumfries Arms' stables, but latterly became garages. The first complete building to the left of this was, and remains, the premises of the Royal Bank of Scotland. The building was erected in 1866 to plans by Peddie & Kinnear. To the left of the bank was the building that originally was a house, built by William MacLatchie, joiner. Its lower floors were later converted into two shop premises. The lighter-coloured building with the two turrets on the facade was erected in 1934 as the Cumnock branch of Auchinleck Co-operative Society. The building was designed by W. F. Valentine.

The buildings between the old co-operative and the Craighead Inn were demolished to allow the widening of Glaisnock Street and the erection of the Glaisnock shopping centre, probably one of the biggest mistakes in Cumnock's town-centre development. Proposals made in 2010 intended returning much of the streetscape, but no doubt not with so fine looking frontages.

HOTEL ROYAL
CHEMIST

The Square & Royal Hotel

A view that has hardly changed in the memories of most Cumnockians, this picture was taken from the start of Glaisnock Street looking back into the Square. Centrally placed is the Old Parish Church, the building dating from 1866, when it was erected by the 3rd Marquis of Bute to plans by James Maitland Wardrop. It is unfortunate that the clock tower was unfinished, for originally it was intended having a spire continuing upwards, which would have been a major landmark for the town.

The Royal Hotel stands to the right, the present building erected around 1892. At the time the hotel was the property of Robert J. Barrowman (d. 1924), whose initials appear on the tympanum over the main entrance doorway. Built of red sandstone, the hotel was for many years known as the Hotel Royal. Prior to the sandstone building there was an older Hotel Royal on the site, a simpler building. The present hotel incorporates the old Eagle Inn, located in the Square. From 1956 the hotel was owned by Stevensons' of Changue until 2001 when it was sold to Robert Kyle.

The building on the left was the Commercial Bank of Scotland, which opened in Cumnock around 1920, the bank agent being R. D. Hunter (d. 1941). Originally, there was a rectangular block here, long occupied by the Hunter family, which had a grocery business up until 1875. It was then converted to an ironmongery by William Hunter. The firm was also noted for its 'Ballochmyle' brand of pedal cycles.

The premises shown were erected in 1927, the new sandstone building having a curved frontage which allowed the traffic easier access to and from the Square. In 1959 the Commercial Bank amalgamated with the National Bank to form the National Commercial Bank. It was taken over by the Royal Bank of Scotland in 1969 and, soon after, this branch was closed. It remains the offices of R. D. Hunter, solicitor and estate agents, currently agent for the Scottish Building Society. Previously, the old vernacular block had been the post office for a time.

Glaisnock Street

Looking north down Glaisnock Street, this photograph shows the centre of town as it was in the 1950s. The narrow stretch of Glaisnock Street with the various vans and lorries shows why it was deemed a good idea at the time to demolish the buildings on the right and widen the road, with considerable loss of much of Cumnock's fine architecture.

On the left is the Bank of Scotland building, erected in 1871-2, to plans by Peddie & Kinnear. The Bank of Scotland first opened a branch in Cumnock on 2 May 1838, when an agency was operated by Hamilton Rose, writer, and Matthew MacKerrow, cloth merchant. Originally the bank operated from MacKerrow's house, but he retired in 1863. In 1868, when Mr Rose retired, it was decided to look for new premises, and it was decided that with the growth of the town, a new purpose-built banking hall should be erected. The site was acquired in 1870 and the bank opened to its customers in January 1873.The bank remained in this building until the 1980s, when it moved to its current location in Townhead Street. The present building survives, now occupied by a solicitor.

The vacant ground to the left of the bank was at one time occupied by single-storey houses, some of which were converted into small shops. The one adjacent to the bank was occupied by Mrs MacSherrie as a confectioner. Some of these shops were demolished and new shops were erected around 1965, one of which was occupied by the co-operative as a supermarket. Another old cottage, which had been divided into four flats, was rebuilt by Duncan MacRae, electrical engineer, for the sale of electrical appliances, which were becoming much more common in households in the 1960s.

The cafe of Mario Luni is seen at the corner of Ayr Road. This occupied the site of the old toll house, where horse-drawn carts and other vehicles had to pay a toll in order to pass along the roads. Beyond, the Old Church and Royal Hotel are two readily-identified landmarks in the scene.

Meetinghouse Bridge

Better known to most Cumnockians as the bridge at the Dubb, this old photograph shows the spot where the Lugar and Glaisnock waters merge. Some say that Cumnock means 'the meeting of the waters', and therefore this is the spot to which it refers. Others, however, claim that the name means 'little shrine', or 'hollow in the hills'. The Dubb is often thought to be one of the deepest pools on the Lugar, but its bed has been altered over the years.

Prior to the construction of Ayr Road and Glaisnock Street, the main road from Cumnock to Ayr came this way. From the Square vicinity, the main road came down Tower Street and Townfoot towards this bridge. The road then struck west, following the present western extension of Ayr Road, towards Ochiltree. Originally the Glaisnock Water was crossed by the Dubb Ford, the name 'dubb' being old Scots for pool or puddle. The first bridge was erected in the eighteenth century, named the Meetinghouse Bridge after the adjacent church, which originally was a simpler building or 'meeting house' where members of the Burgher church worshipped from 1775. The present bridge replaced the old bridge in 1964.

When the members of the kirk wanted to build the church the Marquis of Bute refused to sell them ground, but this site was acquired from John Murdoch. Sand was also refused from the local quarries, but the Glaisnock flooded, dumping sand in the new foundations, an act of providence which was deemed the 'Cumnock miracle'. The first minister of the church, Rev James Hall (1757-1826), was friendly with Robert Burns, and the poet visited him on occasion and stayed overnight at his manse in Auchinleck Road. The church building in the picture was erected in 1831, its simple architecture being typical of Scots 'box kirk' style. The church became a United Presbyterian, United Free and then a Church of Scotland building, known as the West Kirk, but it was closed in 1949 when the congregation merged with the Crichton Memorial Church in Ayr Road, whose spire is seen behind the tree. The building is currently The Box House, a cafe and bar.

Cumnock Free Church

In May 1843 the Church of Scotland had a major split nationally, resulting in 474 ministers leaving to set up the Free Church of Scotland. The problem had been the issue of patronage, the right of local landowners to decide on who should be appointed minister, a choice denied the congregation who had to put up with him, if they didn't like him. Almost every parish congregation was rent in two, and in Cumnock Rev Ninian Bannatyne left the church to form the new congregation.

The Free Church nationally had to build hundreds of churches in as short a period as possible, and as a result used a number of standard plans. Accordingly, the church built in Cumnock was to one of these, and it is noteworthy that the Free Church built in New Cumnock was of the exact same design. The architect was probably David Cousin, who had been employed by the Free Church to produce the standard plans. The building was erected on ground in Ayr Road, from the foundation to the opening taking only six months, being opened on the last Sunday of October 1843. Rev Ninian Bannatyne remained in the pulpit for thirty-one years. It was he who wrote the parish contribution to the *New Statistical Account of Scotland.*

Adjoining the Free Church was the Free Church School, opened in 1844. At the time of the Disruption, education was still in the control of the church, and as the local schoolmaster in Cumnock, John MacKinnel, had become a Free Church adherent, he had to leave his job and house. He became the new dominie at the Free Church School, serving there until retiring in 1862. In 1853 there were 176 pupils in the school.

The third minister of the Free Church was Rev John Warrick, who was ordained in 1883. He wrote a number of books, including *The History of Old Cumnock*, published in 1899.

The old Free Church was demolished in the summer of 1896 following the donation of funds by the Crichton family to allow the erection of the new Crichton Memorial Church, which survives today as Old Cumnock Trinity Church.

Old Parish Church

The present Old Parish Church in the Square has stood there since 1866, but it is known that there have been at least two previous churches on the same site, perhaps more. Only the last two buildings survive in illustrations, and this is probably the only real view of the predecessor building to exist.

The church shown was erected in 1754 to replace an even older building that had become too small for the congregation. When it had been erected is not known, but one of the earliest references to a church in Cumnock probably dates from the middle ages, when the patronage of the parish was transferred by the baron to the Cathedral of Glasgow, who supplied a vicar.

The church in the photograph was built by the local landowner, the 5th Earl of Dumfries, who had been erecting a new country house for himself west of the town, Dumfries House, to replace the ancient Leifnoreis, or Lochnorris Castle. Lord Dumfries had engaged the architects John and Robert Adam to design his new house, and he took the opportunity to have the Adams design a new church at the same time.

The style of the church was fairly simple, a cruciform shape in plan, the low tower with the spire on the south front, the Dumfries burial vault on the north side. Between the two was a single-storey hipped-roof building, with simple arched windows. On the walls were the jougs, where malefactors could be locked up, and shutters on the walls, which were closed to prevent damage to the windows when the local sport of hand-ball was played. Originally the church had 700 sittings, but in 1822 new balconies were erected inside, accessed from external stairs added to either end, increasing the capacity.

In the bell tower was a cast bell dated 1697, the work of Quirinus de Visscher of Rotterdam. On the border is a hunting scene, farming scene, and a church with a tower. The bell was for many years hung on the Bell Tree in the Strand, before being erected in the parish school in 1876. In 1974, when the school was demolished, it was returned to the church, where it is on display in the vestibule.

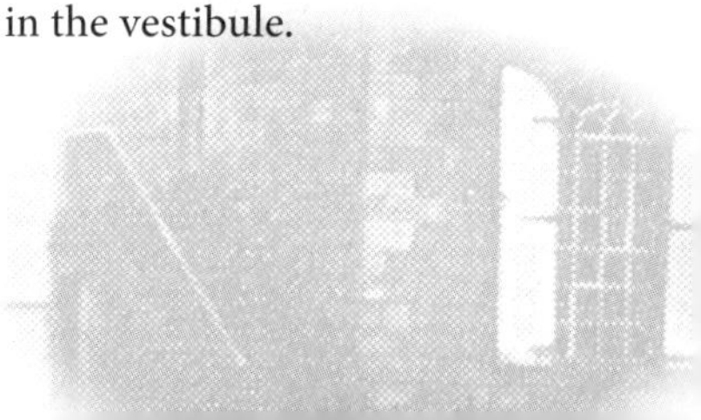

Logan House

The housing estate of Logan dates from 1948, when Ayr County Council purchased Logan House and immediate policies in order to build 307 new homes for miners relocated from the demolished rows in Lugar and Cronberry. In the midst of the scheme stood Logan House, an old country house that had been the property of the Logan family historically. Its site is now occupied by the flats at 18-24A Holmhead Crescent. The old stable block was located where the present Glenmuir Arms is.

Logan was a small estate that was originally owned by the Logan family. The earliest reference to the lands dates from 1600, when George Logan of that Ilk was the laird. The Logans remained in possession until 1798, when Hugh Logan of that Ilk (1731-1802) had to sell up, having lost a considerable fortune in the Ayr Bank Crash of 1772. Hugh Logan was a noted wit and local celebrity. He was known to Robert Burns, who described him as 'Squire Hugh' in his verses. Hugh Logan had the Laird's Pillar erected near to the house, an erect slab of stone that remained long after the house had been demolished. When he died he was buried in Cumnock's Square, the last person to be buried there.

Hugh Logan probably also started the erection of the house, but his financial difficulties probably meant that he was unable to complete it, for it is known to have been unfinished in 1802.

After the Logans the estate was acquired by the Allason family, followed by the Allason-Cunninghames. William Allason-Cunninghame of Logan was the owner of a collection of Burns' manuscripts known as the Afton Collection, now at Burns' Birthplace Museum. It was also he who donated the clock to the Old Church in Cumnock in 1872.

The estate passed to the Bannatyne-Allason family, but they let the house to a variety of tenants. In 1925 the house and 70 acres were sold to Charles Alexander Sadler, but the house was uninhabited by the time of the Second World War and it was demolished in 1949-50.

Cumnock Public School

From the Reformation in 1560 until 1872 education was the job of the church, and it was decreed that a school should be established in every parish. A school in Cumnock came into being soon after the Reformation, perhaps held in the church itself for a time, the earliest reference to it dating from 1625. It was later located at the corner of Lugar Street with Bank Lane, and in 1804 a new school was erected on the north side of the Square, perhaps replacing the old tollbooth of the burgh, the site now occupied by the Clydesdale Bank. The schoolmaster at the time of the new school was William Simson (1758-1815), who was known to Robert Burns as 'Winsome Willie' and whose grave is in the Old Cemetery on Barrhill Road.

In May 1847 a new school was built at Broombrae, on Barrhill Road, and this served the parish until the Public School illustrated was erected and opened to the first scholars on 6 October 1876. David Scott, the master at the Parish School walked with his pupils into the new building, and on the following day Robert Brown brought his from the Former Free Church School in Ayr Road. A new Education Act had been passed in 1872 and following this many new schools were erected across the country. The building was designed by the Kilmarnock architect Robert S. Ingram, though it is thought that the plan was based loosely on that devised by William Lambie Moffat, often copied as being an ideal layout for such schools. The foundation stone was laid on 19 August 1875, the building being erected of red Ballochmyle sandstone at a cost of £2,700. The old Quirinus de Visscher bell that had hung in the bell tree for many years was inserted in the belfry.

The new school was described as one of the 'finest in the south of Scotland', but within a short time it was too small, and a second building was added behind it.

The school was replaced by a new primary school, erected at Green Mill, near Bankend in 1969 and it was eventually demolished around 1974, the old bell being saved beforehand. The extension of 1905 survives, now occupied by Yipworld, a youth information project.

MacCartney's Engineering Works

Situated by the side of the Glaisnock Water, reached from Glaisnock Street by Greenholm Road, was George MacCartney's Engineering Works. There was an old building immediately adjacent to the Glaisnock, the works at one time powered by the stream, and next to it this purpose-built factory was erected, sometime in the first half of the nineteenth century. George MacCartney established his works in 1812, originally at Clocklownie farm, on the road to Benston. In 1832 he moved to Burnside where he commenced manufacture of a variety of metal and steel objects, from agricultural machinery to castings, often used in mills. One of the business's main products was threshing mills, one hundred of these being made each year, selling at £80 each. MacCartney's also made bridges, including the Rifleman's Bridge at Longhouse.

George MacCartney died unmarried in 1868 aged 78 and was buried in Ochiltree. In 1901 MacCartney's was acquired by Charles and Andrew Taylor, who started making electrical switchgear that was used in mines and factories. To increase the flow of water to their works, a new dam seven feet in height was constructed across the Glaisnock Water. The engineering works, however, could not keep up with mass-manufacture, and eventually MacCartney's was closed in 1933.

After MacCartney's works closed, the building was used for a time by Marion Reid who ran it as a model lodging house, a place where the homeless or poor could find a bed for the night. It was later taken over by the local council, who had a joinery here. The building was destroyed by fire on Saturday 17 April 1993, and was subsequently demolished.

Linking MacCartney's works with Townhead Street was an old wooden bridge, but this was washed away in a flood in 1898. It was replaced by an iron bridge, named Betty's Bridge after Elizabeth Howatson, who had been washed away in the flood but was rescued. The old building on the left was originally Glaisnock Cottage, home in 1840 to Charles Howatson, banker. However, it gradually fell into decay, being used as a workshop and store.

CUMNOCK
2M50
D 1853

Cumnock Railway Station

The railway from Glasgow was built as far as Auchinleck in 1848, swinging east to Muirkirk to serve the ironworks there. The large stone-built Bank Viaduct was erected in 1850 across the Lugar Water allowing the railway to continue to Cumnock, and subsequently down Nithsdale to link with the railway at Dumfries. This viaduct has thirteen arches, was designed by John Miller, and the central arch is 175 feet above the level of the river, making it the highest masonry arch in Britain. Old Cumnock Station was opened on 20 May 1850. Built at the east end of the town, reached from Barrhill Terrace, the station had a stationmaster's house, platforms, and sidings.

This photograph was taken from the southbound platform looking almost due west. On the left is the wooden kiosk, with the stationmaster's house behind. In addition, the station had an engine shed beyond, with seven sidings. At the far end of the station area, just short of the Bank Viaduct, was a signal box.

A second station was opened at the top of Glaisnock Street on 1 July 1872 on the Ayr and Edinburgh line, which was located on the south side of the town. A second viaduct, the Glaisnock Viaduct, was constructed across the Glaisnock Water. The station was closed to passengers in 1951, and in 1964 freight trains ceased on the line too. For many years a railway bridge was located at the top end of Glaisnock Street, but this was demolished in 1965.

In the 1960s Dr Richard Beeching was charged by the government with trying to make the nationalised railways profitable, and he decided to close many branch lines and hundreds of stations across the country. Cumnock was to suffer in these cuts, the original station being closed in 1966.

Today the site of the station is occupied by Bute House care home. Little remains to indicate that it was at one time a busy station. Cumnock New Station is similarly gone – the track lifted and the line landscaped away, the flats of George MacTurk Court being erected on the site.

STOPPER
McC's

Looking down Lugar Street

A fairly modern view of Lugar Street as seen from the Square, most of the buildings on the right hand side have been demolished. The first on the right was the Tup Inn, an old hostelry that was long ago occupied by James Tear, followed by his daughter, Janet Riddell. It was then taken over by Matthew Riggans followed by John Tear. Next door (and which latterly became part of the inn) was a bakery, occupied by Marion MacInnes. She also sold vegetables and supplied soup to school children. Her daughter, also Marion, assisted her. The business was continued by Mrs James Neil and afterwards by her daughter, Mrs Reid. It was then occupied (1961) by Miss Stewart as a remnant shop. The Tup Inn was said to be haunted by a young girl, perhaps a maid, who occupied the room above the front lounge. The sound of her was often heard in the 1970s. The inn was demolished without permission on Sunday, 10 November 2002, the owner later fined for this.

The building beyond, with the gable facing the street, was originally a house, but for many years was A. Little's radio and television shop. The lane adjacent to it is Kilnholm Place, in 1914 the location of sixteen houses. Between the two world wars, the lane was the subject of slum clearances, the occupiers rehoused in new council houses. The double-storey white house was Rosebank.

The double-storey building on the left of the street was built as Robert Livingstone's grocery shop, perhaps around 1880. Livingstone's was a long-established firm in the town, Janet Livingstone starting it in 1861. Her son, Robert followed, then James. Livingstone's was a licensed wine, spirit and ale dealer, and for a time sold their own blend of whisky, 'Lugar Blend', named after the local watercourse.

Robert Livingstone built a new house for himself, sometime after 1857. Millbank House was erected in what had been one of the manse fields. It remained a house until it was purchased by Cumnock District Council in 1931 and used as their offices. At the time of writing it is occupied as a local council office and registrar's office.

Some residents of Waterside Place

There have been a number of old streets and lanes in Cumnock that have been removed due to redevelopment over the years. Among these are Elbow Lane, Waterside Row, Manse Lane, Kilnholm Place, Donaldson Braes and Waterside Place. This last-named street was located alongside the Glaisnock Water, access to the street being from Townhead Street.

Waterside Place was a heavily populated part of the town, the houses being tightly packed between the water and the lane. There were no gardens, and the residents had to share various facilities, such as the wash-house. In 1914, just before the First World War, there were a total of 42 houses in the lane, owned by four different landlords – Douglas Duncan, grocer, Thomas Hunter, seedsman, Jesse Allan, farmer's wife, and the trustees of the late David Smith. Thomas Hunter had a store and office for his seed and grain merchant's business. The houses were occupied by various people, such as miners, labourers, bakers, shoemakers, bottlers, and even a dentist's agent.

The first fire station in Cumnock was located here – a shed for a barrow and a hose, erected in 1876. Keir Hardie had his first home in Cumnock here in 1879.

The condition of the houses degenerated considerably between the wars, and developments in modern life meant that they failed to meet the relevant standards expected by tenants. Eventually, the street became subject to one of Cumnock's various 'slum-clearance' schemes. The residents were offered new council houses that were being erected around the hub of the old town, in places such as Drumbrochan, the Hearth, Keir Hardie Hill or the Racecourse. In 1934 the slum clearance scheme targeted 32 houses in Waterside Place, as well as five at Donaldson Braes (off Greenholm Road), four at Holmhead and eighteen others elsewhere in the town.

When the houses of Waterside Place were demolished, the site was left vacant for a number of years and in 1949 was developed for use as a car park. Today, the site of the street is taken by the Glaisnock Shopping Centre and its surroundings.

POLICE
GB
VS 9511

Townhead Street & the Police Station

This old photograph of Townhead Street was taken looking west, towards the parish church. The only buildings in this picture which survive are the said church, and the buildings seen under its tower, with the sun shades out. Townhead Street was originally one of Cumnock's principal thoroughfares, the road from the town centre that led to both Edinburgh and Dumfries. This was before the Barrhill Road was created and the new Glaisnock Street replaced the old route that went by way of Barshare and Craigens, to rejoin the New Cumnock road.

The double-storey building on the right is the old police station and court house. This was erected in 1839 as a court house to replace the old J.P. court which was located in the Square. In 1858 Ayr County Constabulary was created, and the police station was established within the same building. A new court house was added to the rear of the old one in 1895. The police station continued to operate until 1971 when the new police station and district court was erected in Ayr Road. The present police station was opened on Wednesday 29 November 1972 by county councillor James Jennings. It had cost £125,000 to build, the architect being Clark Fyfe. A tall radio mast was completed in October 1971, the topmost segment being positioned by helicopter.

To the left of the police station in the picture is the former wooden hall used by the Salvation Army. It was erected in 1925 on the site of old single-storey cottages. The Salvation Army first set up in Cumnock in 1882 and quickly established a following. By the 1960s the corps had an estimated membership of 75, with around forty members regularly attending services. The corps was still strong enough to plan ahead, and in the 1960s were able to acquire a new site further east in Townhead Street, and there erected a brick-built hall, its roof a flattish butterfly style. On the front wall, facing the street, was a large army badge. This hall, too, has been demolished.

Townhead Street Developments

This photograph shows work starting on the redevelopment of Townhead Street in the 1970s. The vacant ground was the site of old cottages seen to the left of the Salvation Army hall in the last picture. The Salvation Army headquarters can be seen to the left in this picture. The first building on the right was occupied by David White, painter and joiner, followed by John Boyd, joiner, and then Jack Ferguson, dentist. Behind this building was a small engineering works, owned by Montgomerie & Howat. The yard, as well as the gap behind the lorry, was taken over by J. K. Thomson, who operated a car sales garage there, a business that still continues in Barrhill Road.

At the time of the picture, the light coloured building was occupied by M. Blackwood, who had a fishing and shooting supplies shop. Previously this was a bakery, originally operated by Shedden, Clark and latterly by Messrs Gilmour.

An old single-storey house follows to the left, at one time thatched, as were most of the old cottages in Townhead Street. To its left is Crichton Place, a red sandstone building that was demolished in September 2010, some of the stone retained to erect new walls around the Town Hall grounds. The building was originally erected by Charles Crichton, an engineer in Liverpool, but let to various tenants – in 1914 these included Charles Murdoch, postman, William Jackson, baker, and John Hessett, labourer. In more recent years part of the building was used as an architect's office.

To the left of Crichton Place was an old double-storey building, owned by James Murdoch, draper in Ayr, and let to three tenants. It was later to be used by the district council.

Not one single part of this scene survives, Crichton Place being the last building to go. The vacant ground in the picture was where four shops and the Bank of Scotland were built, with the unemployment benefit offices upstairs. The site of the buildings on the far side of the street are partially occupied by the Glaisnock Shopping Centre.

CLYDESDALE
&
OF SCOTLAND BANK
LIMITED
LITTLE

Lugar Street from Lugar Bridge

Taken from the Lugar Bridge in 1961, this photograph shows almost the full length of Lugar Street. This has always been one of the main routes into Cumnock, the principal one from the north. At one time the Lugar Water was crossed by a ford here, often referred to as Stepends Ford. By the early eighteenth century the locals started to demand that a bridge be built. However, it was not until 1752 that one was planned. In 1753 the contract to build the bridge was given to Thomas Brown, who had built Irvine Bridge. He had also built Melrose Bridge in 1753-4, which fell shortly afterwards. The same fate happened to Lugar Bridge, which fell during construction work, four men and four boys being killed. The bridge was later rebuilt.

Lugar Bridge was widened in 2006-7, funded by the Scottish Executive. The parapet on the upstream side was dismantled to just below the string course level. The bridge was widened, a new sandstone abutment and arch was erected, and the original string-course and parapet was re-erected.

The houses on the right, with the dormer windows, were demolished with the light-coloured building to make way for a wider Tanyard. The light coloured building was known as the Jeannie House, erected in the late eighteenth century by Margaret, Countess of Dumfries, as a workshop for the weaving of woollens and linen. It was in ruins in 1914, but the building was later occupied as a house, at one time by Hugh Lorimer. He was something of an antiquarian, and wrote *A Corner of Old Strathclyde*, published in 1952, which looked back at the very early history of the district, especially through place-names.

On the left side of the street the railings around the garden of Riverside House are seen, behind them an old cottage and then Rosebank, both demolished to allow the new link road onto Barrhill Road. A. Little's shop sold radios and televisions in the 1960s. It was previously occupied by the Vallance family as a house and in recent years by a music shop, hairdresser and currently an estate agent.

ROAD
WORKS
AHEAD

Demolition of Castlehill Building

Built in the gusset of Townhead Street and Waterside Place, the Castlehill Building was erected in 1903 to plans by Robert Ingram. It stood on the site of some older buildings, one of which had its gable-end to the street, similar to the Craighead Inn. The old building was home to Mrs MacSherrie, who had a small shop dedicated to children's clothing and remnants. She was also noted for taking in orphan children and bringing them up. Old maps indicate that this building was also known as 'Castlehill', perhaps an elusive reference to some sort of fortified building that may have stood hereabouts. The other building that was demolished to allow the corner building was a bakehouse, operated by 'Batchie' Smith.

The demolished building in the picture was erected by the Muir family, the long-standing firm of Alex Muir & Son being located in Townhead Street. It was founded in 1859 by Alex Muir, who came from Paisley, as a grocery, but he was also noted for his 'Corsegellioch Blend' of whisky. This was a blend of Ardbeg, Islay and Cambus malts, and it sold at sixpence per gill, 'either as a beverage, a stimulant or for Medicinal purposes.' Bottles of it were sold to various places, and even as far afield as England, according to old adverts! Muir's had a branch shop in Muirkirk. Muir was also one of nine local businessmen who signed a petition in 1866 which led to the formation of Cumnock as a Police Burgh in that year. Alex Muir died in 1886, and the firm was taken over by his son James (died 1914), followed by his grandson, Alexander. The business was closed in April 1964, Alex Muir having died a week beforehand. Muir's shop was located at 9 Townhead Street, but they also owned a number of cottages in Waterside Place and the Strand.

The photograph was taken when redevelopment work commenced prior to the erection of the Glaisnock Shopping Centre. Many old premises and houses were cleared away at that time, including some architecturally interesting buildings in Glaisnock Street, and some old sites and workshops in Townhead Street.

AUCHINLECK
Margaret Lindsay.
ALEXANDER McKECHNIE LTD.
PRINTER, BOOKSELLER & STATIONER
LIPTON
TACKLE
SHOWROOM
ILFORD
Ayr A 70
Dumfries
A 76
CYCLE
RACE

Glaisnock Street

Taken when a cycle race was passing through the centre of town, this photograph shows the shops on the east side of Glaisnock Street, most of which have been demolished. In fact, the only building that survives is the former branch of the Auchinleck Co-operative Society. This building was erected in 1933 and officially opened on 20 January 1934 by William Kerr, president of the society. It was designed by the architect W. F. Valentine of Kilmarnock. Previously a plain vernacular double-storey building stood there, with two small shops in it.

Auchinleck Co-operative Society was formed in 1890, and became one of the largest societies locally. It had branches in Cumnock and Ochiltree, as well as in various local miners' rows. The last co-operative shop in Cumnock, located in Hamilton Place, closed in 2009.

To the left of the co-op was Margaret Lindsay's clothes shop, the shop previously occupied by Turnbull and Allan, watchmakers. At one time a well-known public clock was located on the middle of this building. When the watchmaking shop closed in 1918, the clock was put up for sale. The cost of £10 was gifted by an anonymous native. It was repaired in 1920 and lit at the same time. It was later revealed that the late R. Stewart Bain, living in London, had paid for the clock. In July 1963 a double-decker bus hit it, knocking it from the wall. A new clock was acquired, erected on the co-operative in 1965.

Next to the left was Alexander MacKechnie's, printer, bookseller and stationer. This building had been erected in 1863 by Duncan Ballantine, a printer and bookseller, whose business was taken over by MacKechnie.

Left again, the light-coloured frontage was used as a storeroom by Lipton's grocery, which follows further left. Originally the store was a grocery in its own right, occupied successively by William Duncan, John Vallance, Gillespie & Smith, James Rae, and the Wilsons. Lipton, a branch of a large chain famed for its tea, occupied a shop that had previously been run by local drapers, including, Mr MacKinnell, William Bryson and David Balsillie, 'cash drapers'.

Townhead Street

This old photograph shows the buildings at the middle part of Townhead Street, where the roadway drops considerably. All of the buildings have been demolished, the only ones that survive being those in the far distance, the council houses of upper Townhead Street and Elizabeth Crescent. They were erected in 1953, the latter street named after the newly-crowned queen.

The small shop on the left was a tobacconist and sweetshop, advertising Senior Service. This was at one time Jimmy Wardrop's fishing tackle shop. The sudden drop in the road level is roughly where there is a cross marked out on the roadway with stone cobbles. This marks the site where the market cross stood for a time. Originally the cross appears to have been located in the north-east corner of the Square, in front of what is now the Mercat Hotel, but when the Square was changed from a graveyard into an open thoroughfare, the cross became something of a restriction to traffic flow, and it was relocated here. In later years the cross was returned to the Square, being positioned in front of the church door, but it was relocated once more to its present position in the widest corner of the Square.

Many of the old cottages in this part of the town were originally occupied by weavers, but in later years they were taken over by miners who worked in some of the local mines. The Townhead pit was located further along the street, the trees on the right being planted on it. At one time a bogey line led from the Townhead pit up the steep hill to the Barrhill pits, all of which were owned by the same company, Messrs. Freeland and Lancaster. This firm went bankrupt in 1849 and they were taken over by the Portland Iron Company of Hurlford.

Some of the houses at this end of the street included Moodie's Row, erected in 1902 by James Moodie, grocer, and other blocks owned by Marion Baird, Annie Murray and George Reid of Catrine. The site of the houses to the left is now occupied by the houses numbered 73-85 Towhead Street. Just behind the pole at one time was a public well.

CUBBIN
Wm CARLE
A76
A70
J. CLIMIE
PRINTERS & STATIONERS
R. STODDART
SENIOR SERVICE

The Gorbals

This view of Glaisnock Street is taken from the Royal Hotel and looks south, up the street towards the site of Cumnock Pottery. This part of the street is known as the Gorbals, the bridge across the Glaisnock Water being called Gorbals Bridge. Most of the buildings on the right survive, though the occupants of all have changed. The only one bearing the same name, however, is D. Connell & Co., printers and stationers, but this has moved to the shop next door. Connells is an old-established company in the town, originally producing postcards and booklets. The shop to the right was J. Patterson's, a general merchant.

To the left of Connell's was John Climie's butcher's shop, the firm being established in 1850. Climie's and Connell's shops are built on top of the Glaisnock, forming part of the Gorbals Bridge. These premises were erected sometime after 1857, for prior to that the bridge was a typical structure with a parapet to the downstream side. The upstream side had been built over before 1857, the building on the left occupied by William MacCubbin and William Carle straddling the water.

Beyond Climie's was Robert Stoddart's bakery, and left again, in the same building, was another of Climie's shops, this one a confectioner. The building further left, with the projecting sign, was the Buck's Head Inn. On 10 June 1833 a murder took place here, when a meeting of farmers was being held to discuss the difficulty of local poaching. Some poachers had been caught, and were held here. The meeting was repeatedly interrupted by local poachers, who were trying to free their friends, and the warning was given that the next to enter the room would be shot! Unfortunately, David Reid of Barshare farm, who had turned up late for the meeting, entered next, and was shot by Robert Collins, gamekeeper on the Ballochmyle estate. Collins couldn't live with what he had done. Nine months later he was shot by his own gun, it supposedly having gone off whilst he cleaned it. It may have been suicide. He left a widow with a young family.

AA
HOTEL
RAC
BAKERY and DAIRY
RESTAURANT
CRA

Black Bull Close

At one time the lane here was a main route in the centre of Cumnock. Prior to the Square opening to traffic, this was the roadway that linked the main street of the village – Townfoot and Townhead – with the manse to the north. The buildings now occupied by the Royal and Mercat hotels faced the other way round, onto the lane, turning their back on the graveyard. In time, the buildings were redesigned or rebuilt, and the Black Bull Close became a back lane.

On the left is the Royal Hotel, seen here sometime after 1964, when Stevenson's had opened their bakery shop on the ground floor. The bakehouse was located up a close to the right, now occupied by the Royal Bar. The hotel had extended across the close, the double-storey bridge now being reduced to a single storey. On the right of the close is J. MacCall's licensed betting office. This was at one time the Wheatsheaf Inn, and before that it was known as the Loudoun Arms.

The building being demolished was John MacGavin's bakery. John MacGavin established his business in Cumnock in 1837, moving here from Sorn. On the Flemish-style gable is a small shield with a date, perhaps reading 1838, and possibly the work of James Ingram. MacGavin was famous for making 'Cumnock Tarts', a local delicacy of apple or rhubarb filling in a pastry case, thickly coated with glazed sugar. The site of this building is now the Royal Hotel car park.

On the right, sporting its black and white painted finish, is the Craighead Inn. This building had a lease drawn up on 20 March 1722 in which the annual rent was '£21 together with 2 hens in January or February and to the house of Leifnoreis two loads of coal yearly.' In 1915 the local fire-cart was stored in a shed here. Various hosts at the inn over the years included John Reid in the early 1900s. He sold his own 'Craighead Blend' of old Highland malt whiskies. The inn also sold the cheaper Glenmuir Water blend of whisky.

ELECTRICITY BOARD
SERVICE
CENTRE
McJANNET
GROCERS
McJANNET.

The Square at the Pawn Steps Corner

The south west corner of the Square is where the Pawn Steps are located, hidden in this old photograph. The steps led down from the Square to Bank Lane, and the top of Townfoot, now part of Tower Street. The Pawn Steps were often used to describe the location of various businesses within the town, for example, in a newspaper advert of 1934, 'the old firm' of Gillespie & Sons, did not give its proper address, preferring instead to direct customers 'down the pawn stairs'. Many other older Cumnock residents often referred to locations 'at the fit o' the pawn steps.'

The scene is very similar today, apart from the fact that the central building has been demolished. On the immediate left, the white-coloured building was Nan MacGrady's shoe shop. The Electricity Board shop is located in what is one of Cumnock's finest examples of late eighteenth century buildings. It follows the traditional manner of having large first floor windows, and lesser ones above.

In the demolished building were two shop premises, at the time of the picture being taken these being occupied by James MacIntyre, grocer, and the office of the Greenan Laundry. Previously, the laundry shop was occupied by David Brown Cree, who operated it as a pawnbroker, and from which business the steps no doubt got their name. It was later occupied by Andrew 'Dusky' MacCall as a restaurant.

The building to the right of the close is known as Clydesdale House, as it was here that the Clydesdale Bank first opened for business in Cumnock. The building was sold in 1807, the titles of the time being transferred from William Howat to James Baird. The Ayrshire Banking Company purchased the building in 1834, passing to the Western Bank of Scotland in 1845-7, and to the Clydesdale Bank in 1857. It is thought that the Western Bank erected the present building around 1845-7. In 1883, when the Clydesdale Bank moved to its present site on the north side of the Square, the building was sold to David Cree.

Clydesdale House was long occupied by Messrs. MacJannet, who had a grocery store there. It is now occupied by a Chinese restaurant and a barber.

Acknowledgments

I would like to thank a variety of people who have kindly supplied pictures that have been used in this book. They include the *Cumnock Chronicle*, Elizabeth Stevenson, and Robert Young. The other pictures are part of the author's own collection of images. I would also like to thank the many people who have supplied information to me over the years. Often these notes are filed away, to be used at some time in the future.